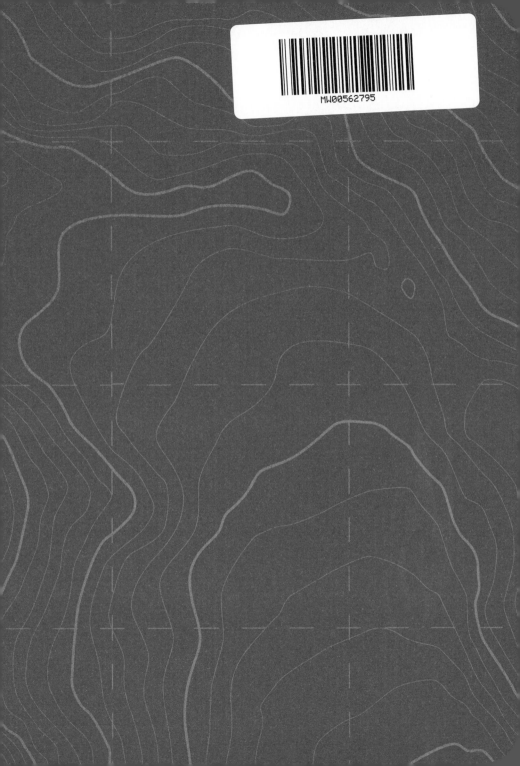

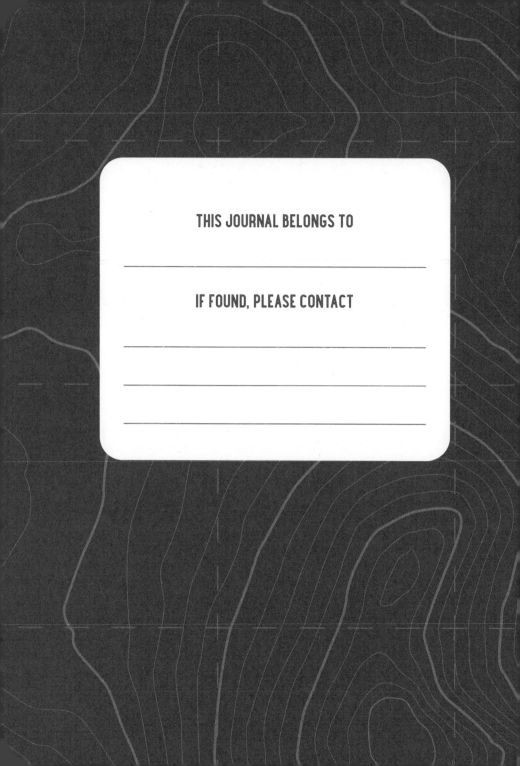

THIS JOURNAL BELONGS TO

_____

IF FOUND, PLEASE CONTACT

_____

_____

_____

THE HIKING LOGBOOK

RECORD YOUR ADVENTURES

PETER PAUPER PRESS, INC.
WHITE PLAINS, NEW YORK

**PETER PAUPER PRESS**
*Fine Books and Gifts Since 1928*

### Our Company

In 1928, at the age of twenty-two, Peter Beilenson began printing books on a small press in the basement of his parents' home in Larchmont, New York. Peter—and later, his wife, Edna—sought to create fine books that sold at "prices even a pauper could afford."

Today, still family owned and operated, Peter Pauper Press continues to honor our founders' legacy—and our customers' expectations—of beauty, quality, and value.

Designed by Margaret Rubiano

Written by Barbara Paulding

Images used under license from Shutterstock.com

Visit us at www.peterpauper.com

U se this logbook as a record of your hiking life, from your favorite hikes to spots you'd rather avoid, as well as standout memories of your time in nature. Recall where and when you had that incredible wildlife sighting, or encountered tricky conditions and had to turn back. Write down the details of your adventures so you can remember clearly and share or revisit favorite trails. Follow the prompts to note information such as trail name and location, duration and distance, hiking companions, observations, and highlights.

# HIKING RULES

Relax—you're on nature time • Unplug your life • Walk in the sunshine •
Hike more, worry less • Hug a tree • Breathe deeply • Be a happy hiker •
Leave nothing but footprints • Take nothing but pictures •
Kill nothing but time

**TRAIL** ............................................................................................ **DATE** ...................

Location ............................................................................................................

Weather ☀ ⛅ ☁ ⛅ 🌧 ⛈ ☁ 🌨 🌧  Temperature ...................

Duration and distance ............................ Time of day ............................

Type of hike  ☐ Loop  ☐ Out and back  ☐ One way

Terrain ............................................................................................................

Trail conditions ............................................................................................

Other hikers on the trail  ☐ Many  ☐ Some  ☐ Few  ☐ None

Difficulty level  ☐ Easy  ☐ Moderate  ☐ Strenuous

Hiking companion(s) ......................................................................................

Facilities ......................................................................................................

☐ First visit  ☐ Return hike  ☐ Would hike again

Observations (wildlife, trees and other flora, geology, views, rivers and lakes)

............................................................................................................

............................................................................................................

............................................................................................................

Trail pros and cons ......................................................................................

............................................................................................................

............................................................................................................

Things to remember for next time ..............................................................

............................................................................................................

Highlights ....................................................................................................

............................................................................................................

Rate your hike  ★ ★ ★ ★ ★

# NOTES AND PICTURES

**TRAIL** ............................................................................................ **DATE** ..................

Location .........................................................................................................

Weather ☀ ⛅ ☁ 🌤 🌦 ⛈ ☁ 🌨 🌨 Temperature ......................

Duration and distance ........................... Time of day ............................

Type of hike  ☐ Loop  ☐ Out and back  ☐ One way

Terrain ..........................................................................................................

Trail conditions ............................................................................................

Other hikers on the trail  ☐ Many  ☐ Some  ☐ Few  ☐ None

Difficulty level  ☐ Easy  ☐ Moderate  ☐ Strenuous

Hiking companion(s) ......................................................................................

Facilities ........................................................................................................

☐ First visit  ☐ Return hike  ☐ Would hike again

Observations (wildlife, trees and other flora, geology, views, rivers and lakes)

...................................................................................................................

...................................................................................................................

...................................................................................................................

Trail pros and cons ........................................................................................

...................................................................................................................

...................................................................................................................

Things to remember for next time ...............................................................

...................................................................................................................

Highlights ......................................................................................................

...................................................................................................................

Rate your hike  ★ ★ ★ ★ ★

# NOTES AND PICTURES

**TRAIL** ........................................................................................ **DATE** ...............

Location .....................................................................................................................

Weather ☀️ ⛅ ☁️ 🌤️ 🌦️ ⛈️ 🌥️ ☁️ 🌨️ Temperature ...................

Duration and distance............................Time of day................................

Type of hike ☐ Loop ☐ Out and back ☐ One way

Terrain ......................................................................................................................

Trail conditions ......................................................................................................

Other hikers on the trail ☐ Many ☐ Some ☐ Few ☐ None

Difficulty level ☐ Easy ☐ Moderate ☐ Strenuous

Hiking companion(s)...............................................................................................

Facilities.....................................................................................................................

☐ First visit ☐ Return hike ☐ Would hike again

Observations (wildlife, trees and other flora, geology, views, rivers and lakes)

.....................................................................................................................................

.....................................................................................................................................

.....................................................................................................................................

Trail pros and cons.................................................................................................

.....................................................................................................................................

.....................................................................................................................................

Things to remember for next time.......................................................................

.....................................................................................................................................

Highlights..................................................................................................................

.....................................................................................................................................

Rate your hike ★ ★ ★ ★ ★

# NOTES AND PICTURES

**TRAIL** ......................................................................................................................... **DATE** ..............

Location .........................................................................................................................................

Weather ☀ ⛅ ☁ 🌤 🌧 ⛈ ☁ 🌨 🌨 Temperature ..............

Duration and distance................................Time of day ................................

Type of hike  ☐ Loop  ☐ Out and back  ☐ One way

Terrain ..........................................................................................................................................

Trail conditions ........................................................................................................................

Other hikers on the trail  ☐ Many  ☐ Some  ☐ Few  ☐ None

Difficulty level  ☐ Easy  ☐ Moderate  ☐ Strenuous

Hiking companion(s).................................................................................................................

Facilities.......................................................................................................................................

☐ First visit  ☐ Return hike  ☐ Would hike again

Observations (wildlife, trees and other flora, geology, views, rivers and lakes)

.......................................................................................................................................................

.......................................................................................................................................................

.......................................................................................................................................................

Trail pros and cons.....................................................................................................................

.......................................................................................................................................................

.......................................................................................................................................................

Things to remember for next time..........................................................................................

.......................................................................................................................................................

Highlights.....................................................................................................................................

.......................................................................................................................................................

Rate your hike  ★ ★ ★ ★ ★

# NOTES AND PICTURES

**TRAIL** ............................................................................................................. **DATE** ..................

Location ...............................................................................................................................

Weather ☀ ⛅ ☁ 🌤 🌧 ⛈ ☁ 🌨 🌧  Temperature ...................

Duration and distance.............................Time of day...................................

Type of hike  ☐ Loop  ☐ Out and back  ☐ One way

Terrain ................................................................................................................................

Trail conditions .................................................................................................................

Other hikers on the trail  ☐ Many  ☐ Some  ☐ Few  ☐ None

Difficulty level  ☐ Easy  ☐ Moderate  ☐ Strenuous

Hiking companion(s).........................................................................................................

Facilities.............................................................................................................................

☐ First visit  ☐ Return hike  ☐ Would hike again

Observations (wildlife, trees and other flora, geology, views, rivers and lakes)

.............................................................................................................................................

.............................................................................................................................................

.............................................................................................................................................

Trail pros and cons...........................................................................................................

.............................................................................................................................................

.............................................................................................................................................

Things to remember for next time.................................................................................

.............................................................................................................................................

Highlights...........................................................................................................................

.............................................................................................................................................

Rate your hike  ★ ★ ★ ★ ★

# NOTES AND PICTURES

**TRAIL** .................................................................................................. **DATE** ..................

Location ........................................................................................................................

Weather ☀️ ⛅ ☁️ 🌤️ 🌧️ ⛈️ ☁️ 🌨️ 🌧️ Temperature ..................

Duration and distance ........................................ Time of day ..............................

Type of hike  ☐ Loop  ☐ Out and back  ☐ One way

Terrain ........................................................................................................................

Trail conditions ........................................................................................................

Other hikers on the trail  ☐ Many  ☐ Some  ☐ Few  ☐ None

Difficulty level  ☐ Easy  ☐ Moderate  ☐ Strenuous

Hiking companion(s) ..................................................................................................

Facilities ....................................................................................................................

☐ First visit  ☐ Return hike  ☐ Would hike again

Observations (wildlife, trees and other flora, geology, views, rivers and lakes)

........................................................................................................................

........................................................................................................................

........................................................................................................................

Trail pros and cons ..................................................................................................

........................................................................................................................

........................................................................................................................

Things to remember for next time ..........................................................................

........................................................................................................................

Highlights ..................................................................................................................

........................................................................................................................

Rate your hike  ★ ★ ★ ★ ★

# NOTES AND PICTURES

**TRAIL** ............................................................................................ **DATE** ...........................

Location ...................................................................................................................

Weather ☀ ⛆ ☁ ⛅ ☁ ⛈ ☁ ☁ ☃ Temperature ...........................

Duration and distance.........................Time of day.........................

Type of hike ☐ Loop   ☐ Out and back   ☐ One way

Terrain ....................................................................................................................

Trail conditions .....................................................................................................

Other hikers on the trail   ☐ Many   ☐ Some   ☐ Few   ☐ None

Difficulty level   ☐ Easy   ☐ Moderate   ☐ Strenuous

Hiking companion(s)...........................................................................................

Facilities...............................................................................................................

☐ First visit   ☐ Return hike   ☐ Would hike again

Observations (wildlife, trees and other flora, geology, views, rivers and lakes)

.............................................................................................................................

.............................................................................................................................

.............................................................................................................................

Trail pros and cons..............................................................................................

.............................................................................................................................

.............................................................................................................................

Things to remember for next time.......................................................................

.............................................................................................................................

Highlights...............................................................................................................

.............................................................................................................................

Rate your hike   ★ ★ ★ ★ ★

# NOTES AND PICTURES

**TRAIL** ........................................................................................... **DATE** ...................

Location ....................................................................................................................

Weather ☀ 🌦 ☁ 🌤 🌧 ⛈ ☁ 🌨 🌨 Temperature ...................

Duration and distance........................................Time of day ...........................

Type of hike  ☐ Loop    ☐ Out and back    ☐ One way

Terrain .....................................................................................................................

Trail conditions .....................................................................................................

Other hikers on the trail  ☐ Many   ☐ Some   ☐ Few   ☐ None

Difficulty level  ☐ Easy   ☐ Moderate   ☐ Strenuous

Hiking companion(s)...............................................................................................

Facilities...................................................................................................................

☐ First visit   ☐ Return hike   ☐ Would hike again

Observations (wildlife, trees and other flora, geology, views, rivers and lakes)

....................................................................................................................

....................................................................................................................

....................................................................................................................

Trail pros and cons.................................................................................................

....................................................................................................................

....................................................................................................................

Things to remember for next time..........................................................................

....................................................................................................................

Highlights................................................................................................................

....................................................................................................................

Rate your hike   ★ ★ ★ ★ ★

# NOTES AND PICTURES

**TRAIL** ........................................................................................ **DATE** ..........................

Location ...........................................................................................................................

Weather ☀ ⛅ ☁ 🌤 🌦 ⛈ ☁ 🌨 🌨 Temperature ..........................

Duration and distance ........................... Time of day ...........................

Type of hike  ☐ Loop  ☐ Out and back  ☐ One way

Terrain ...........................................................................................................................

Trail conditions ...........................................................................................................

Other hikers on the trail  ☐ Many  ☐ Some  ☐ Few  ☐ None

Difficulty level  ☐ Easy  ☐ Moderate  ☐ Strenuous

Hiking companion(s) ....................................................................................................

Facilities ......................................................................................................................

☐ First visit  ☐ Return hike  ☐ Would hike again

Observations (wildlife, trees and other flora, geology, views, rivers and lakes)

..........................................................................................................................................

..........................................................................................................................................

..........................................................................................................................................

Trail pros and cons ......................................................................................................

..........................................................................................................................................

..........................................................................................................................................

Things to remember for next time ..............................................................................

..........................................................................................................................................

Highlights .....................................................................................................................

..........................................................................................................................................

Rate your hike  ★ ★ ★ ★ ★

# NOTES AND PICTURES

**TRAIL** ............................................................................................ **DATE** ..................

Location ...........................................................................................................

Weather ☀ ⛅ ☁ ⛅ 🌧 ⛈ ☁ 🌨 🌨 Temperature ........................

Duration and distance........................Time of day ........................

Type of hike ☐ Loop ☐ Out and back ☐ One way

Terrain ...........................................................................................................

Trail conditions .............................................................................................

Other hikers on the trail ☐ Many ☐ Some ☐ Few ☐ None

Difficulty level ☐ Easy ☐ Moderate ☐ Strenuous

Hiking companion(s)........................................................................................

Facilities.......................................................................................................

☐ First visit ☐ Return hike ☐ Would hike again

Observations (wildlife, trees and other flora, geology, views, rivers and lakes)

...........................................................................................................

...........................................................................................................

...........................................................................................................

Trail pros and cons.........................................................................................

...........................................................................................................

...........................................................................................................

Things to remember for next time......................................................................

...........................................................................................................

Highlights.......................................................................................................

...........................................................................................................

Rate your hike ★ ★ ★ ★ ★

# NOTES AND PICTURES

**TRAIL** ......................................................................................................... **DATE** ...................

Location ..........................................................................................................................

Weather ☀️ ⛅ ☁️ 🌤️ ☁️ ⛈️ ☁️ ☁️ 🌨️ Temperature..............................

Duration and distance............................Time of day.......................................

Type of hike   ☐ Loop   ☐ Out and back   ☐ One way

Terrain ...........................................................................................................................

Trail conditions ...........................................................................................................

Other hikers on the trail   ☐ Many   ☐ Some   ☐ Few   ☐ None

Difficulty level   ☐ Easy   ☐ Moderate   ☐ Strenuous

Hiking companion(s)......................................................................................................

Facilities........................................................................................................................

☐ First visit   ☐ Return hike   ☐ Would hike again

Observations (wildlife, trees and other flora, geology, views, rivers and lakes)

.............................................................................................................................

.............................................................................................................................

.............................................................................................................................

Trail pros and cons.........................................................................................................

.............................................................................................................................

.............................................................................................................................

Things to remember for next time.....................................................................................

.............................................................................................................................

Highlights........................................................................................................................

.............................................................................................................................

Rate your hike   ★ ★ ★ ★ ★

# NOTES AND PICTURES

**TRAIL** ......................................................................................................... **DATE** ..............................

Location ....................................................................................................................................

Weather ☀ ⛅ ☁ ⛅ 🌧 ⛈ ☁ 🌨 🌨 Temperature ...........................

Duration and distance.........................................Time of day ..............................................

Type of hike  ☐ Loop  ☐ Out and back  ☐ One way

Terrain .....................................................................................................................................

Trail conditions .....................................................................................................................

Other hikers on the trail  ☐ Many  ☐ Some  ☐ Few  ☐ None

Difficulty level  ☐ Easy  ☐ Moderate  ☐ Strenuous

Hiking companion(s)............................................................................................................

Facilities.................................................................................................................................

☐ First visit  ☐ Return hike  ☐ Would hike again

Observations (wildlife, trees and other flora, geology, views, rivers and lakes)

...................................................................................................................................................

...................................................................................................................................................

...................................................................................................................................................

Trail pros and cons...............................................................................................................

...................................................................................................................................................

...................................................................................................................................................

Things to remember for next time....................................................................................

...................................................................................................................................................

Highlights................................................................................................................................

...................................................................................................................................................

Rate your hike  ★ ★ ★ ★ ★

# NOTES AND PICTURES

**TRAIL** .................................................................................................. **DATE** ....................

Location ...............................................................................................................

Weather ☀ 🌤 ☁ ⛅ 🌦 ⛈ 🌧 🌨 🌧 Temperature ....................

Duration and distance...............................Time of day.......................

Type of hike  ☐ Loop  ☐ Out and back  ☐ One way

Terrain ..................................................................................................

Trail conditions ....................................................................................

Other hikers on the trail  ☐ Many  ☐ Some  ☐ Few  ☐ None

Difficulty level  ☐ Easy  ☐ Moderate  ☐ Strenuous

Hiking companion(s)................................................................................

Facilities................................................................................................

☐ First visit  ☐ Return hike  ☐ Would hike again

Observations (wildlife, trees and other flora, geology, views, rivers and lakes)

.............................................................................................................

.............................................................................................................

.............................................................................................................

Trail pros and cons..................................................................................

.............................................................................................................

.............................................................................................................

Things to remember for next time.............................................................

.............................................................................................................

Highlights...............................................................................................

.............................................................................................................

Rate your hike  ★ ★ ★ ★ ★

# NOTES AND PICTURES

**TRAIL** .................................................................................................... **DATE** ...............

Location ...........................................................................................................................

Weather ☀ ⛅ ☁ 🌤 🌧 ⛈ 🌧 ☁ 🌨 Temperature ................

Duration and distance.......................................Time of day...............................

Type of hike ☐ Loop ☐ Out and back ☐ One way

Terrain ...........................................................................................................................

Trail conditions .........................................................................................................

Other hikers on the trail ☐ Many ☐ Some ☐ Few ☐ None

Difficulty level ☐ Easy ☐ Moderate ☐ Strenuous

Hiking companion(s)....................................................................................................

Facilities.......................................................................................................................

☐ First visit ☐ Return hike ☐ Would hike again

Observations (wildlife, trees and other flora, geology, views, rivers and lakes)

..........................................................................................................................................

..........................................................................................................................................

..........................................................................................................................................

..........................................................................................................................................

Trail pros and cons......................................................................................................

..........................................................................................................................................

..........................................................................................................................................

Things to remember for next time...............................................................................

..........................................................................................................................................

Highlights......................................................................................................................

..........................................................................................................................................

Rate your hike ★ ★ ★ ★ ★

# NOTES AND PICTURES

**TRAIL** ........................................................................................................ **DATE** ....................

Location ................................................................................................................................

Weather ☀ ⛅ ☁ ⛅ 🌧 ⛈ ☁ 🌨 🌨 Temperature ....................

Duration and distance........................................Time of day ....................................

Type of hike ☐ Loop ☐ Out and back ☐ One way

Terrain ....................................................................................................................

Trail conditions ......................................................................................................

Other hikers on the trail ☐ Many ☐ Some ☐ Few ☐ None

Difficulty level ☐ Easy ☐ Moderate ☐ Strenuous

Hiking companion(s)................................................................................................

Facilities................................................................................................................

☐ First visit ☐ Return hike ☐ Would hike again

Observations (wildlife, trees and other flora, geology, views, rivers and lakes)

....................................................................................................................................

....................................................................................................................................

....................................................................................................................................

Trail pros and cons................................................................................................

....................................................................................................................................

....................................................................................................................................

Things to remember for next time............................................................................

....................................................................................................................................

Highlights..............................................................................................................

....................................................................................................................................

Rate your hike ★ ★ ★ ★ ★

# NOTES AND PICTURES

**TRAIL** .................................................. **DATE** ............

Location ...............................................................................

Weather ☀️ 🌦️ ☁️ ⛅ 🌧️ ⛈️ ☁️ 🌨️ 🌨️ Temperature ............

Duration and distance ........................ Time of day ...............

Type of hike   ☐ Loop   ☐ Out and back   ☐ One way

Terrain ..............................................................................

Trail conditions ..................................................................

Other hikers on the trail   ☐ Many   ☐ Some   ☐ Few   ☐ None

Difficulty level   ☐ Easy   ☐ Moderate   ☐ Strenuous

Hiking companion(s) .............................................................

Facilities ............................................................................

☐ First visit   ☐ Return hike   ☐ Would hike again

Observations (wildlife, trees and other flora, geology, views, rivers and lakes)

.......................................................................................

.......................................................................................

.......................................................................................

Trail pros and cons ...............................................................

.......................................................................................

.......................................................................................

Things to remember for next time .............................................

.......................................................................................

Highlights ...........................................................................

.......................................................................................

Rate your hike   ★   ★   ★   ★   ★

# NOTES AND PICTURES

**TRAIL** ........................................................................................................ **DATE** ...............

Location ...........................................................................................................................

Weather ☀ ⛅ ☁ ⛅ 🌧 ⛈ 🌦 🌨 🌨 Temperature .................

Duration and distance ............................... Time of day ...............................

Type of hike ☐ Loop ☐ Out and back ☐ One way

Terrain ............................................................................................................................

Trail conditions ...........................................................................................................

Other hikers on the trail ☐ Many ☐ Some ☐ Few ☐ None

Difficulty level ☐ Easy ☐ Moderate ☐ Strenuous

Hiking companion(s) ...................................................................................................

Facilities .......................................................................................................................

☐ First visit ☐ Return hike ☐ Would hike again

Observations (wildlife, trees and other flora, geology, views, rivers and lakes)

.......................................................................................................................................

.......................................................................................................................................

.......................................................................................................................................

Trail pros and cons ....................................................................................................

.......................................................................................................................................

.......................................................................................................................................

Things to remember for next time ...........................................................................

.......................................................................................................................................

Highlights ......................................................................................................................

.......................................................................................................................................

Rate your hike  ★  ★  ★  ★  ★

# NOTES AND PICTURES

**TRAIL** ......................................................................... **DATE** ..................

Location ..............................................................................................

Weather ☀ ⛅ ☁ 🌤 🌧 ⛈ ☁ 🌨 🌨 Temperature ..................

Duration and distance ........................... Time of day ....................

Type of hike  ☐ Loop   ☐ Out and back   ☐ One way

Terrain ...............................................................................................

Trail conditions ...............................................................................

Other hikers on the trail  ☐ Many  ☐ Some  ☐ Few  ☐ None

Difficulty level  ☐ Easy  ☐ Moderate  ☐ Strenuous

Hiking companion(s) .........................................................................

Facilities ...........................................................................................

☐ First visit   ☐ Return hike   ☐ Would hike again

Observations (wildlife, trees and other flora, geology, views, rivers and lakes)

...............................................................................................................

...............................................................................................................

...............................................................................................................

Trail pros and cons ..........................................................................

...............................................................................................................

...............................................................................................................

Things to remember for next time .................................................

...............................................................................................................

Highlights ..........................................................................................

...............................................................................................................

Rate your hike  ★ ★ ★ ★ ★

# NOTES AND PICTURES

**TRAIL** ....................................................................................................... **DATE** ...................

Location .............................................................................................................................

Weather ☀ ⛅ ☁ 🌤 🌧 ⛈ 🌥 ☁ 🌨 Temperature ...................

Duration and distance.................................... Time of day ...............................

Type of hike  ☐ Loop  ☐ Out and back  ☐ One way

Terrain .............................................................................................................................

Trail conditions .............................................................................................................

Other hikers on the trail  ☐ Many  ☐ Some  ☐ Few  ☐ None

Difficulty level  ☐ Easy  ☐ Moderate  ☐ Strenuous

Hiking companion(s).......................................................................................................

Facilities ..........................................................................................................................

☐ First visit  ☐ Return hike  ☐ Would hike again

Observations (wildlife, trees and other flora, geology, views, rivers and lakes)

.............................................................................................................................

.............................................................................................................................

.............................................................................................................................

Trail pros and cons.........................................................................................................

.............................................................................................................................

.............................................................................................................................

Things to remember for next time..................................................................................

.............................................................................................................................

Highlights.........................................................................................................................

.............................................................................................................................

Rate your hike  ★ ★ ★ ★ ★

# NOTES AND PICTURES

**TRAIL** ........................................................................................................ **DATE** ................................

Location ......................................................................................................................................

Weather ☀ ⛅ ☁ 🌤 🌧 ⛈ ☁ 🌨 🌨 Temperature ........................

Duration and distance ........................................ Time of day ........................................

Type of hike ☐ Loop ☐ Out and back ☐ One way

Terrain ........................................................................................................................................

Trail conditions ........................................................................................................................

Other hikers on the trail ☐ Many ☐ Some ☐ Few ☐ None

Difficulty level ☐ Easy ☐ Moderate ☐ Strenuous

Hiking companion(s) ................................................................................................................

Facilities ....................................................................................................................................

☐ First visit ☐ Return hike ☐ Would hike again

Observations (wildlife, trees and other flora, geology, views, rivers and lakes)

........................................................................................................................................

........................................................................................................................................

........................................................................................................................................

Trail pros and cons ..................................................................................................................

........................................................................................................................................

........................................................................................................................................

Things to remember for next time ..........................................................................................

........................................................................................................................................

Highlights ..................................................................................................................................

........................................................................................................................................

Rate your hike ★ ★ ★ ★ ★

# NOTES AND PICTURES

**TRAIL** ............................................................................ **DATE** ................................

Location ...........................................................................................................................

Weather ☀ ⛅ ☁ 🌤 ☁ ⛈ ☁ 🌨 🌨 Temperature ..............................

Duration and distance .............................. Time of day ..............................

Type of hike ☐ Loop ☐ Out and back ☐ One way

Terrain .............................................................................................................................

Trail conditions ............................................................................................................

Other hikers on the trail ☐ Many ☐ Some ☐ Few ☐ None

Difficulty level ☐ Easy ☐ Moderate ☐ Strenuous

Hiking companion(s) ....................................................................................................

Facilities ..........................................................................................................................

☐ First visit ☐ Return hike ☐ Would hike again

Observations (wildlife, trees and other flora, geology, views, rivers and lakes)

........................................................................................................................................

........................................................................................................................................

........................................................................................................................................

Trail pros and cons .......................................................................................................

........................................................................................................................................

........................................................................................................................................

Things to remember for next time .............................................................................

........................................................................................................................................

Highlights ........................................................................................................................

........................................................................................................................................

Rate your hike ★ ★ ★ ★ ★

# NOTES AND PICTURES

**TRAIL** ........................................................................................................ **DATE** ...............

Location .............................................................................................................................

Weather ☀ ⛅ ☁ 🌤 ⛈ 🌧 ☁ 🌨 ❄ Temperature ...................

Duration and distance................................Time of day ...............................

Type of hike  ☐ Loop    ☐ Out and back    ☐ One way

Terrain ...............................................................................................................................

Trail conditions ..........................................................................................................

Other hikers on the trail  ☐ Many  ☐ Some  ☐ Few  ☐ None

Difficulty level  ☐ Easy  ☐ Moderate  ☐ Strenuous

Hiking companion(s).................................................................................................

Facilities........................................................................................................................

☐ First visit  ☐ Return hike  ☐ Would hike again

Observations (wildlife, trees and other flora, geology, views, rivers and lakes)

...........................................................................................................................................

...........................................................................................................................................

...........................................................................................................................................

...........................................................................................................................................

Trail pros and cons..................................................................................................

...........................................................................................................................................

...........................................................................................................................................

Things to remember for next time......................................................................

...........................................................................................................................................

Highlights.....................................................................................................................

...........................................................................................................................................

Rate your hike  ★  ★  ★  ★  ★

# NOTES AND PICTURES

**TRAIL** ............................................................................................ **DATE** ..............

Location ............................................................................................

Weather ☀ ⛅ ☁ 🌤 🌧 ⛈ ☁ 🌨 🌨 Temperature ..............

Duration and distance ...................................... Time of day ..............

Type of hike ☐ Loop ☐ Out and back ☐ One way

Terrain ............................................................................................

Trail conditions ............................................................................................

Other hikers on the trail ☐ Many ☐ Some ☐ Few ☐ None

Difficulty level ☐ Easy ☐ Moderate ☐ Strenuous

Hiking companion(s) ............................................................................................

Facilities ............................................................................................

☐ First visit ☐ Return hike ☐ Would hike again

Observations (wildlife, trees and other flora, geology, views, rivers and lakes)

............................................................................................

............................................................................................

............................................................................................

Trail pros and cons ............................................................................................

............................................................................................

............................................................................................

Things to remember for next time ............................................................................................

............................................................................................

Highlights ............................................................................................

............................................................................................

Rate your hike ★ ★ ★ ★ ★

# NOTES AND PICTURES

**TRAIL** ......................................................................................................... **DATE** ...............................

Location ...........................................................................................................................

Weather ☀ ⛅ ☁ ⛅ 🌧 ⛈ ☁ 🌨 🌨 Temperature ...............

Duration and distance.............................Time of day.............................................

Type of hike ☐ Loop  ☐ Out and back  ☐ One way

Terrain .............................................................................................................

Trail conditions ...............................................................................................

Other hikers on the trail ☐ Many ☐ Some ☐ Few ☐ None

Difficulty level ☐ Easy ☐ Moderate ☐ Strenuous

Hiking companion(s)........................................................................................

Facilities.........................................................................................................

☐ First visit ☐ Return hike ☐ Would hike again

Observations (wildlife, trees and other flora, geology, views, rivers and lakes)

.........................................................................................................................

.........................................................................................................................

.........................................................................................................................

Trail pros and cons...........................................................................................

.........................................................................................................................

.........................................................................................................................

Things to remember for next time...................................................................

.........................................................................................................................

Highlights.........................................................................................................

.........................................................................................................................

Rate your hike ★ ★ ★ ★ ★

# NOTES AND PICTURES

**TRAIL** ........................................................................ **DATE** ..................

Location ................................................................................................

Weather ☀ ⛅ ☁ 🌤 🌧 ⛈ ☁ 🌨 🌨 Temperature ..................

Duration and distance........................Time of day...........................

Type of hike  ☐ Loop  ☐ Out and back  ☐ One way

Terrain ..................................................................................................

Trail conditions ....................................................................................

Other hikers on the trail  ☐ Many  ☐ Some  ☐ Few  ☐ None

Difficulty level  ☐ Easy  ☐ Moderate  ☐ Strenuous

Hiking companion(s)...............................................................................

Facilities...............................................................................................

☐ First visit  ☐ Return hike  ☐ Would hike again

Observations (wildlife, trees and other flora, geology, views, rivers and lakes)

................................................................................................

................................................................................................

................................................................................................

Trail pros and cons................................................................................

................................................................................................

................................................................................................

Things to remember for next time............................................................

................................................................................................

Highlights.............................................................................................

................................................................................................

Rate your hike  ★ ★ ★ ★ ★

# NOTES AND PICTURES

**TRAIL** .................................................................................................................. **DATE** ............................

Location .........................................................................................................................................

Weather ☀ ⛅ ☁ 🌤 🌧 ⛈ ☁ 🌨 🌨 Temperature ..........................

Duration and distance ................................... Time of day ..........................................

Type of hike  ☐ Loop   ☐ Out and back   ☐ One way

Terrain ..........................................................................................................................................

Trail conditions .........................................................................................................................

Other hikers on the trail  ☐ Many   ☐ Some   ☐ Few   ☐ None

Difficulty level  ☐ Easy   ☐ Moderate   ☐ Strenuous

Hiking companion(s) ...............................................................................................................

Facilities ......................................................................................................................................

☐ First visit   ☐ Return hike   ☐ Would hike again

Observations (wildlife, trees and other flora, geology, views, rivers and lakes)

....................................................................................................................................................

....................................................................................................................................................

....................................................................................................................................................

....................................................................................................................................................

Trail pros and cons ...................................................................................................................

....................................................................................................................................................

....................................................................................................................................................

Things to remember for next time ........................................................................................

....................................................................................................................................................

Highlights ....................................................................................................................................

....................................................................................................................................................

Rate your hike   ★ ★ ★ ★ ★

# NOTES AND PICTURES

**TRAIL** ........................................................................................ **DATE** ...................................

Location ..............................................................................................................................

Weather ☀ ⛅ ☁ 🌤 🌧 ⛈ ☁ 🌨 🌨 Temperature ...........................

Duration and distance........................................ Time of day........................................

Type of hike ☐ Loop ☐ Out and back ☐ One way

Terrain ...............................................................................................................................

Trail conditions ................................................................................................................

Other hikers on the trail ☐ Many ☐ Some ☐ Few ☐ None

Difficulty level ☐ Easy ☐ Moderate ☐ Strenuous

Hiking companion(s)..........................................................................................................

Facilities.............................................................................................................................

☐ First visit ☐ Return hike ☐ Would hike again

Observations (wildlife, trees and other flora, geology, views, rivers and lakes)

..............................................................................................................................................

..............................................................................................................................................

..............................................................................................................................................

..............................................................................................................................................

Trail pros and cons.............................................................................................................

..............................................................................................................................................

..............................................................................................................................................

Things to remember for next time......................................................................................

..............................................................................................................................................

Highlights..........................................................................................................................

..............................................................................................................................................

Rate your hike ★ ★ ★ ★ ★

# NOTES AND PICTURES

**TRAIL** ........................................................................................ **DATE** ...............

Location ...................................................................................................................

Weather ☀ ⛅ ☁ ⛅ 🌧 ⛈ ☁ 🌨 🌨 Temperature ...............

Duration and distance....................... Time of day ...............................

Type of hike ☐ Loop ☐ Out and back ☐ One way

Terrain ........................................................................................................................

Trail conditions .......................................................................................................

Other hikers on the trail ☐ Many ☐ Some ☐ Few ☐ None

Difficulty level ☐ Easy ☐ Moderate ☐ Strenuous

Hiking companion(s)..................................................................................................

Facilities..................................................................................................................

☐ First visit ☐ Return hike ☐ Would hike again

Observations (wildlife, trees and other flora, geology, views, rivers and lakes)

.......................................................................................................................................

.......................................................................................................................................

.......................................................................................................................................

Trail pros and cons...................................................................................................

.......................................................................................................................................

.......................................................................................................................................

Things to remember for next time...........................................................................

.......................................................................................................................................

Highlights...................................................................................................................

.......................................................................................................................................

Rate your hike ★ ★ ★ ★ ★

# NOTES AND PICTURES

**TRAIL** ........................................................................................ **DATE** ..........................

Location ................................................................................................................

Weather ☀ ⛅ ☁ ⛅ 🌧 ⛈ ☁ 🌨 🌧 Temperature ..................

Duration and distance.............................Time of day ..................................

Type of hike  ☐ Loop  ☐ Out and back  ☐ One way

Terrain ................................................................................................................

Trail conditions ...................................................................................................

Other hikers on the trail  ☐ Many  ☐ Some  ☐ Few  ☐ None

Difficulty level  ☐ Easy  ☐ Moderate  ☐ Strenuous

Hiking companion(s)..............................................................................................

Facilities.............................................................................................................

☐ First visit  ☐ Return hike  ☐ Would hike again

Observations (wildlife, trees and other flora, geology, views, rivers and lakes)

................................................................................................................

................................................................................................................

................................................................................................................

Trail pros and cons...............................................................................................

................................................................................................................

................................................................................................................

Things to remember for next time.............................................................................

................................................................................................................

Highlights.............................................................................................................

................................................................................................................

Rate your hike  ★ ★ ★ ★ ★

# NOTES AND PICTURES

**TRAIL** ........................................................................................ **DATE** .........................................

Location ...........................................................................................................................................

Weather ☀ ⛅ ☁ 🌤 🌥 ⛈ ☁ 🌨 🌨 Temperature........................

Duration and distance........................Time of day..........................................

Type of hike ☐ Loop ☐ Out and back ☐ One way

Terrain ..............................................................................................................................................

Trail conditions ............................................................................................................................

Other hikers on the trail ☐ Many ☐ Some ☐ Few ☐ None

Difficulty level ☐ Easy ☐ Moderate ☐ Strenuous

Hiking companion(s)......................................................................................................................

Facilities............................................................................................................................................

☐ First visit ☐ Return hike ☐ Would hike again

Observations (wildlife, trees and other flora, geology, views, rivers and lakes)

.............................................................................................................................................................

.............................................................................................................................................................

.............................................................................................................................................................

Trail pros and cons.......................................................................................................................

.............................................................................................................................................................

.............................................................................................................................................................

Things to remember for next time...........................................................................................

.............................................................................................................................................................

Highlights..........................................................................................................................................

.............................................................................................................................................................

Rate your hike ★ ★ ★ ★ ★

# NOTES AND PICTURES

**TRAIL** ............................................................................................ **DATE** ...................

Location .................................................................................................................

Weather ☀ ⛅ ☁ ⛅ 🌧 ⛈ ☁ 🌨 🌨 Temperature ...............

Duration and distance.......................................Time of day ..........................................

Type of hike  ☐ Loop  ☐ Out and back  ☐ One way

Terrain ...................................................................................................................

Trail conditions ......................................................................................................

Other hikers on the trail  ☐ Many  ☐ Some  ☐ Few  ☐ None

Difficulty level  ☐ Easy  ☐ Moderate  ☐ Strenuous

Hiking companion(s)................................................................................................

Facilities..................................................................................................................

☐ First visit  ☐ Return hike  ☐ Would hike again

Observations (wildlife, trees and other flora, geology, views, rivers and lakes)

.................................................................................................................................

.................................................................................................................................

.................................................................................................................................

Trail pros and cons...................................................................................................

.................................................................................................................................

.................................................................................................................................

Things to remember for next time............................................................................

.................................................................................................................................

Highlights................................................................................................................

.................................................................................................................................

Rate your hike  ★ ★ ★ ★ ★

# NOTES AND PICTURES

**TRAIL** ......................................................................... **DATE** ..................

Location .................................................................................

Weather ☀ ⛅ ☁ 🌤 🌧 ⛈ ☁ 🌨 🌨 Temperature ..................

Duration and distance.......................... Time of day .......................

Type of hike ☐ Loop ☐ Out and back ☐ One way

Terrain ....................................................................................

Trail conditions ......................................................................

Other hikers on the trail ☐ Many ☐ Some ☐ Few ☐ None

Difficulty level ☐ Easy ☐ Moderate ☐ Strenuous

Hiking companion(s)..................................................................

Facilities.................................................................................

☐ First visit ☐ Return hike ☐ Would hike again

Observations (wildlife, trees and other flora, geology, views, rivers and lakes)

.................................................................................................

.................................................................................................

.................................................................................................

Trail pros and cons..................................................................

.................................................................................................

.................................................................................................

Things to remember for next time..........................................

.................................................................................................

Highlights...............................................................................

.................................................................................................

Rate your hike ★ ★ ★ ★ ★

# NOTES AND PICTURES

**TRAIL** .................................................................................................... **DATE** ...................

Location .......................................................................................................................

Weather ☀️ ⛅ ☁️ 🌤️ 🌧️ ⛈️ 🌥️ 🌨️ 🌨️ Temperature ...................

Duration and distance........................................Time of day...........................

Type of hike ☐ Loop   ☐ Out and back   ☐ One way

Terrain ..........................................................................................................................

Trail conditions ...........................................................................................................

Other hikers on the trail ☐ Many   ☐ Some   ☐ Few   ☐ None

Difficulty level ☐ Easy   ☐ Moderate   ☐ Strenuous

Hiking companion(s)...................................................................................................

Facilities....................................................................................................................

☐ First visit   ☐ Return hike   ☐ Would hike again

Observations (wildlife, trees and other flora, geology, views, rivers and lakes)

.......................................................................................................................................

.......................................................................................................................................

.......................................................................................................................................

.......................................................................................................................................

Trail pros and cons.....................................................................................................

.......................................................................................................................................

.......................................................................................................................................

Things to remember for next time.............................................................................

.......................................................................................................................................

Highlights.....................................................................................................................

.......................................................................................................................................

Rate your hike   ★ ★ ★ ★ ★

# NOTES AND PICTURES

**TRAIL** ............................................................................................................ **DATE** ..................

Location .........................................................................................................................................

Weather ☀ ⛅ ☁ 🌤 🌦 ⛈ ☁ 🌨 🌨 Temperature ......................

Duration and distance ........................................ Time of day ..................................................

Type of hike ☐ Loop ☐ Out and back ☐ One way

Terrain ...........................................................................................................................................

Trail conditions .........................................................................................................................

Other hikers on the trail ☐ Many ☐ Some ☐ Few ☐ None

Difficulty level ☐ Easy ☐ Moderate ☐ Strenuous

Hiking companion(s) ..................................................................................................................

Facilities .......................................................................................................................................

☐ First visit ☐ Return hike ☐ Would hike again

Observations (wildlife, trees and other flora, geology, views, rivers and lakes)

...........................................................................................................................................................

...........................................................................................................................................................

...........................................................................................................................................................

Trail pros and cons ....................................................................................................................

...........................................................................................................................................................

...........................................................................................................................................................

Things to remember for next time .......................................................................................

...........................................................................................................................................................

Highlights ....................................................................................................................................

...........................................................................................................................................................

Rate your hike ★ ★ ★ ★ ★

# NOTES AND PICTURES

**TRAIL** ..................................................................................................... **DATE** ....................

Location ...........................................................................................................................

Weather ☀ 🌧 ☁ ⛅ ☁ ⛈ ☁ ☁ 🌨 Temperature ....................

Duration and distance....................................Time of day ......................................

Type of hike ☐ Loop ☐ Out and back ☐ One way

Terrain ..............................................................................................................................

Trail conditions ............................................................................................................

Other hikers on the trail ☐ Many ☐ Some ☐ Few ☐ None

Difficulty level ☐ Easy ☐ Moderate ☐ Strenuous

Hiking companion(s)......................................................................................................

Facilities...........................................................................................................................

☐ First visit ☐ Return hike ☐ Would hike again

Observations (wildlife, trees and other flora, geology, views, rivers and lakes)

.............................................................................................................................................

.............................................................................................................................................

.............................................................................................................................................

.............................................................................................................................................

Trail pros and cons........................................................................................................

.............................................................................................................................................

.............................................................................................................................................

.............................................................................................................................................

Things to remember for next time.............................................................................

.............................................................................................................................................

.............................................................................................................................................

Highlights.........................................................................................................................

.............................................................................................................................................

Rate your hike ★ ★ ★ ★ ★

# NOTES AND PICTURES

**TRAIL** .................................................................. **DATE** ................

Location ..........................................................................................

Weather ☀ ⛅ ☁ 🌤 🌧 ⛈ ☁ 🌨 🌨 Temperature ................

Duration and distance ........................... Time of day ................

Type of hike ☐ Loop ☐ Out and back ☐ One way

Terrain ..............................................................................................

Trail conditions ............................................................................

Other hikers on the trail ☐ Many ☐ Some ☐ Few ☐ None

Difficulty level ☐ Easy ☐ Moderate ☐ Strenuous

Hiking companion(s) ......................................................................

Facilities .........................................................................................

☐ First visit ☐ Return hike ☐ Would hike again

Observations (wildlife, trees and other flora, geology, views, rivers and lakes)

..........................................................................................................

..........................................................................................................

..........................................................................................................

Trail pros and cons .........................................................................

..........................................................................................................

..........................................................................................................

Things to remember for next time ................................................

..........................................................................................................

Highlights ........................................................................................

..........................................................................................................

Rate your hike ★ ★ ★ ★ ★

# NOTES AND PICTURES

**TRAIL** ........................................................................................ **DATE** ..................

Location ........................................................................................................

Weather ☀️ ⛅ ☁️ 🌤️ 🌧️ ⛈️ 🌥️ ☁️ 🌨️  Temperature ..................

Duration and distance .................................. Time of day ..........................

Type of hike  ☐ Loop  ☐ Out and back  ☐ One way

Terrain ........................................................................................................

Trail conditions ..........................................................................................

Other hikers on the trail  ☐ Many  ☐ Some  ☐ Few  ☐ None

Difficulty level  ☐ Easy  ☐ Moderate  ☐ Strenuous

Hiking companion(s) ....................................................................................

Facilities ....................................................................................................

☐ First visit  ☐ Return hike  ☐ Would hike again

Observations (wildlife, trees and other flora, geology, views, rivers and lakes)

........................................................................................................

........................................................................................................

........................................................................................................

........................................................................................................

Trail pros and cons ......................................................................................

........................................................................................................

........................................................................................................

Things to remember for next time ..................................................................

........................................................................................................

Highlights ..................................................................................................

........................................................................................................

Rate your hike  ★ ★ ★ ★ ★

# NOTES AND PICTURES

**TRAIL** .................................................... **DATE** ..............

Location ....................................................................................

Weather ☀ 🌦 ☁ 🌤 🌧 ⛈ ☁ 🌨 🌨 Temperature ..............

Duration and distance................................Time of day ....................

Type of hike  ☐ Loop   ☐ Out and back   ☐ One way

Terrain ......................................................................................

Trail conditions ........................................................................

Other hikers on the trail  ☐ Many   ☐ Some   ☐ Few   ☐ None

Difficulty level  ☐ Easy   ☐ Moderate   ☐ Strenuous

Hiking companion(s)...................................................................

Facilities...................................................................................

☐ First visit   ☐ Return hike   ☐ Would hike again

Observations (wildlife, trees and other flora, geology, views, rivers and lakes)

....................................................................................

....................................................................................

....................................................................................

Trail pros and cons...................................................................

....................................................................................

....................................................................................

Things to remember for next time..............................................

....................................................................................

Highlights.................................................................................

....................................................................................

Rate your hike   ★ ★ ★ ★ ★

# NOTES AND PICTURES

**TRAIL** ............................................................................................. **DATE** ...............

Location ...........................................................................................................

Weather ☀️ ⛅ ☁️ 🌤️ 🌧️ ⛈️ ☁️ 🌨️ 🌨️ Temperature ...............

Duration and distance.............................. Time of day.............................

Type of hike ☐ Loop ☐ Out and back ☐ One way

Terrain ............................................................................................................

Trail conditions ...............................................................................................

Other hikers on the trail ☐ Many ☐ Some ☐ Few ☐ None

Difficulty level ☐ Easy ☐ Moderate ☐ Strenuous

Hiking companion(s)..........................................................................................

Facilities.........................................................................................................

☐ First visit ☐ Return hike ☐ Would hike again

Observations (wildlife, trees and other flora, geology, views, rivers and lakes)

....................................................................................................................

....................................................................................................................

....................................................................................................................

....................................................................................................................

Trail pros and cons.........................................................................................

....................................................................................................................

....................................................................................................................

Things to remember for next time....................................................................

....................................................................................................................

Highlights........................................................................................................

....................................................................................................................

Rate your hike ★ ★ ★ ★ ★

# NOTES AND PICTURES

**TRAIL** .................................................................................................. **DATE** ..............................

Location ...............................................................................................................................

Weather ☀ ⛅ ☁ 🌤 🌧 ⛈ ☁ ☁ 🌨 Temperature ...........................

Duration and distance........................................Time of day...........................................

Type of hike ☐ Loop ☐ Out and back ☐ One way

Terrain .................................................................................................................................

Trail conditions ...............................................................................................................

Other hikers on the trail ☐ Many ☐ Some ☐ Few ☐ None

Difficulty level ☐ Easy ☐ Moderate ☐ Strenuous

Hiking companion(s)......................................................................................................

Facilities.............................................................................................................................

☐ First visit ☐ Return hike ☐ Would hike again

Observations (wildlife, trees and other flora, geology, views, rivers and lakes)

.................................................................................................................................................

.................................................................................................................................................

.................................................................................................................................................

Trail pros and cons......................................................................................................

.................................................................................................................................................

.................................................................................................................................................

Things to remember for next time.........................................................................

.................................................................................................................................................

Highlights..........................................................................................................................

.................................................................................................................................................

Rate your hike ★ ★ ★ ★ ★

# NOTES AND PICTURES

**TRAIL** ......................................................................................... **DATE** .................

Location .......................................................................................................................

Weather ☀ ⛅ ☁ 🌤 🌦 ⛈ ☁ 🌨 🌧 Temperature.......................

Duration and distance.................................Time of day .....................................

Type of hike ☐ Loop ☐ Out and back ☐ One way

Terrain .........................................................................................................................

Trail conditions ........................................................................................................

Other hikers on the trail ☐ Many ☐ Some ☐ Few ☐ None

Difficulty level ☐ Easy ☐ Moderate ☐ Strenuous

Hiking companion(s)...................................................................................................

Facilities....................................................................................................................

☐ First visit ☐ Return hike ☐ Would hike again

Observations (wildlife, trees and other flora, geology, views, rivers and lakes)

.......................................................................................................................................

.......................................................................................................................................

.......................................................................................................................................

Trail pros and cons...................................................................................................

.......................................................................................................................................

Things to remember for next time............................................................................

.......................................................................................................................................

Highlights...................................................................................................................

.......................................................................................................................................

Rate your hike ★ ★ ★ ★ ★

# NOTES AND PICTURES

**TRAIL** ................................................................................................ **DATE** ..........................

Location ....................................................................................................................................

Weather ☀ ⛅ ☁ 🌤 🌧 ⛈ ☁ 🌨 ☁  Temperature ..........................

Duration and distance........................................ Time of day ..................................

Type of hike  ☐ Loop   ☐ Out and back   ☐ One way

Terrain ....................................................................................................................................

Trail conditions ....................................................................................................................

Other hikers on the trail  ☐ Many   ☐ Some   ☐ Few   ☐ None

Difficulty level  ☐ Easy   ☐ Moderate   ☐ Strenuous

Hiking companion(s)................................................................................................................

Facilities................................................................................................................................

☐ First visit   ☐ Return hike   ☐ Would hike again

Observations (wildlife, trees and other flora, geology, views, rivers and lakes)

....................................................................................................................................

....................................................................................................................................

....................................................................................................................................

Trail pros and cons.................................................................................................................

....................................................................................................................................

....................................................................................................................................

Things to remember for next time.........................................................................................

....................................................................................................................................

Highlights...............................................................................................................................

....................................................................................................................................

Rate your hike   ★ ★ ★ ★ ★

# NOTES AND PICTURES

**TRAIL** ........................................................................................................ **DATE** ................................

Location ........................................................................................................................................

Weather ☀ ⛅ ☁ 🌤 🌧 ⛈ ☁ 🌨 ❄ Temperature ................................

Duration and distance ........................................ Time of day ................................

Type of hike  ☐ Loop  ☐ Out and back  ☐ One way

Terrain ........................................................................................................................

Trail conditions ........................................................................................................

Other hikers on the trail  ☐ Many  ☐ Some  ☐ Few  ☐ None

Difficulty level  ☐ Easy  ☐ Moderate  ☐ Strenuous

Hiking companion(s) ..................................................................................................

Facilities ......................................................................................................................

☐ First visit  ☐ Return hike  ☐ Would hike again

Observations (wildlife, trees and other flora, geology, views, rivers and lakes)

........................................................................................................................................

........................................................................................................................................

........................................................................................................................................

Trail pros and cons ....................................................................................................

........................................................................................................................................

........................................................................................................................................

Things to remember for next time .............................................................................

........................................................................................................................................

Highlights ....................................................................................................................

........................................................................................................................................

Rate your hike  ★ ★ ★ ★ ★

# NOTES AND PICTURES

**TRAIL** ............................................................................................................ **DATE** ...............................

Location ...........................................................................................................................................

Weather ☀️ 🌦️ ☁️ 🌤️ 🌧️ ⛈️ ☁️ ☁️ 🌨️ Temperature ...........................

Duration and distance................................Time of day...........................................................

Type of hike ☐ Loop ☐ Out and back ☐ One way

Terrain ...............................................................................................................................

Trail conditions ...............................................................................................................

Other hikers on the trail ☐ Many ☐ Some ☐ Few ☐ None

Difficulty level ☐ Easy ☐ Moderate ☐ Strenuous

Hiking companion(s)........................................................................................................

Facilities............................................................................................................................

☐ First visit ☐ Return hike ☐ Would hike again

Observations (wildlife, trees and other flora, geology, views, rivers and lakes)

.............................................................................................................................................

.............................................................................................................................................

.............................................................................................................................................

Trail pros and cons.........................................................................................................

.............................................................................................................................................

.............................................................................................................................................

Things to remember for next time...............................................................................

.............................................................................................................................................

Highlights.........................................................................................................................

.............................................................................................................................................

Rate your hike ★ ★ ★ ★ ★

# NOTES AND PICTURES

**TRAIL** ........................................................................................................ **DATE** ................

Location ...............................................................................................................................

Weather ☀ ⛅ ☁ 🌤 🌧 ⛈ 🌥 🌨 🌨 Temperature ...................

Duration and distance ........................... Time of day ................................

Type of hike ☐ Loop   ☐ Out and back   ☐ One way

Terrain ..................................................................................................................................

Trail conditions ...................................................................................................................

Other hikers on the trail ☐ Many   ☐ Some   ☐ Few   ☐ None

Difficulty level ☐ Easy   ☐ Moderate   ☐ Strenuous

Hiking companion(s) ..........................................................................................................

Facilities ..............................................................................................................................

☐ First visit   ☐ Return hike   ☐ Would hike again

Observations (wildlife, trees and other flora, geology, views, rivers and lakes)

.............................................................................................................................................

.............................................................................................................................................

.............................................................................................................................................

.............................................................................................................................................

Trail pros and cons .............................................................................................................

.............................................................................................................................................

.............................................................................................................................................

Things to remember for next time ....................................................................................

.............................................................................................................................................

Highlights .............................................................................................................................

.............................................................................................................................................

Rate your hike ★ ★ ★ ★ ★

# NOTES AND PICTURES

**TRAIL** ......................................................................... **DATE** ................

Location ................................................................................................

Weather ☀ ⛅ ☁ ⛅ 🌧 ⛈ ☁ ☁ 🌨   Temperature ................

Duration and distance ........................... Time of day ...................

Type of hike ☐ Loop   ☐ Out and back   ☐ One way

Terrain ..................................................................................................

Trail conditions ....................................................................................

Other hikers on the trail ☐ Many   ☐ Some   ☐ Few   ☐ None

Difficulty level ☐ Easy   ☐ Moderate   ☐ Strenuous

Hiking companion(s) ............................................................................

Facilities ...............................................................................................

☐ First visit   ☐ Return hike   ☐ Would hike again

Observations (wildlife, trees and other flora, geology, views, rivers and lakes)

...............................................................................................................

...............................................................................................................

...............................................................................................................

...............................................................................................................

Trail pros and cons ..............................................................................

...............................................................................................................

...............................................................................................................

Things to remember for next time ........................................................

...............................................................................................................

Highlights .............................................................................................

...............................................................................................................

Rate your hike ★ ★ ★ ★ ★

# NOTES AND PICTURES

**TRAIL** ........................................................................................................ **DATE** ...........................

Location ....................................................................................................................................

Weather ☀ ⛅ ☁ 🌤 🌧 ⛈ ☁ 🌨 🌨 Temperature ...........................

Duration and distance........................................Time of day ...................................

Type of hike ☐ Loop ☐ Out and back ☐ One way

Terrain ......................................................................................................................

Trail conditions ......................................................................................................

Other hikers on the trail ☐ Many ☐ Some ☐ Few ☐ None

Difficulty level ☐ Easy ☐ Moderate ☐ Strenuous

Hiking companion(s)...............................................................................................

Facilities..................................................................................................................

☐ First visit ☐ Return hike ☐ Would hike again

Observations (wildlife, trees and other flora, geology, views, rivers and lakes)

........................................................................................................................................

........................................................................................................................................

........................................................................................................................................

Trail pros and cons...............................................................................................

........................................................................................................................................

........................................................................................................................................

Things to remember for next time........................................................................

........................................................................................................................................

Highlights................................................................................................................

........................................................................................................................................

Rate your hike ★ ★ ★ ★ ★

# NOTES AND PICTURES

**TRAIL** .................................................................................................. **DATE** ..................

Location ..........................................................................................................................

Weather ☀ ⛅ ☁ 🌤 🌧 ⛈ 🌨 🌨 Temperature ..........................

Duration and distance ........................................ Time of day ..................................

Type of hike  ☐ Loop  ☐ Out and back  ☐ One way

Terrain ..........................................................................................................................

Trail conditions ..........................................................................................................

Other hikers on the trail  ☐ Many  ☐ Some  ☐ Few  ☐ None

Difficulty level  ☐ Easy  ☐ Moderate  ☐ Strenuous

Hiking companion(s) ....................................................................................................

Facilities ......................................................................................................................

☐ First visit  ☐ Return hike  ☐ Would hike again

Observations (wildlife, trees and other flora, geology, views, rivers and lakes)

..........................................................................................................................

..........................................................................................................................

..........................................................................................................................

Trail pros and cons ..................................................................................................

..........................................................................................................................

..........................................................................................................................

Things to remember for next time ............................................................................

..........................................................................................................................

Highlights ..................................................................................................................

..........................................................................................................................

Rate your hike  ★ ★ ★ ★ ★

# NOTES AND PICTURES

**TRAIL** ........................................................................................................ **DATE** ..................

Location ........................................................................................................................

Weather ☀ ⛅ ☁ 🌤 🌧 ⛈ 🌥 🌨 🌨 Temperature ..................

Duration and distance ........................... Time of day ..................................

Type of hike ☐ Loop ☐ Out and back ☐ One way

Terrain ........................................................................................................................

Trail conditions ...........................................................................................................

Other hikers on the trail ☐ Many ☐ Some ☐ Few ☐ None

Difficulty level ☐ Easy ☐ Moderate ☐ Strenuous

Hiking companion(s) .....................................................................................................

Facilities ......................................................................................................................

☐ First visit ☐ Return hike ☐ Would hike again

Observations (wildlife, trees and other flora, geology, views, rivers and lakes)

........................................................................................................................

........................................................................................................................

........................................................................................................................

........................................................................................................................

Trail pros and cons ......................................................................................................

........................................................................................................................

........................................................................................................................

Things to remember for next time .................................................................................

........................................................................................................................

Highlights ....................................................................................................................

........................................................................................................................

Rate your hike ★ ★ ★ ★ ★

# NOTES AND PICTURES

**TRAIL** ........................................................................................ **DATE** ..............

Location ........................................................................................................

Weather ☀️ ⛅ ☁️ 🌦️ 🌦️ ⛈️ ☁️ 🌨️ 🌨️ Temperature ..............

Duration and distance ..............................Time of day ..............................

Type of hike ☐ Loop ☐ Out and back ☐ One way

Terrain ........................................................................................................

Trail conditions ..........................................................................................

Other hikers on the trail ☐ Many ☐ Some ☐ Few ☐ None

Difficulty level ☐ Easy ☐ Moderate ☐ Strenuous

Hiking companion(s) ....................................................................................

Facilities ....................................................................................................

☐ First visit ☐ Return hike ☐ Would hike again

Observations (wildlife, trees and other flora, geology, views, rivers and lakes)

........................................................................................................

........................................................................................................

........................................................................................................

........................................................................................................

Trail pros and cons ....................................................................................

........................................................................................................

........................................................................................................

Things to remember for next time ................................................................

........................................................................................................

Highlights ..................................................................................................

........................................................................................................

Rate your hike ★ ★ ★ ★ ★

# NOTES AND PICTURES

**TRAIL** .................................................................................................................. **DATE** ....................

Location ....................................................................................................................................

Weather ☀ ⛅ ☁ 🌤 🌧 ⛈ 🌥 ☁ 🌨 Temperature ........................

Duration and distance................................................Time of day ....................................

Type of hike ☐ Loop ☐ Out and back ☐ One way

Terrain ....................................................................................................................................

Trail conditions ....................................................................................................................

Other hikers on the trail ☐ Many ☐ Some ☐ Few ☐ None

Difficulty level ☐ Easy ☐ Moderate ☐ Strenuous

Hiking companion(s)............................................................................................................

Facilities................................................................................................................................

☐ First visit ☐ Return hike ☐ Would hike again

Observations (wildlife, trees and other flora, geology, views, rivers and lakes)

....................................................................................................................................

....................................................................................................................................

....................................................................................................................................

Trail pros and cons...............................................................................................................

....................................................................................................................................

....................................................................................................................................

Things to remember for next time.......................................................................................

....................................................................................................................................

Highlights...............................................................................................................................

....................................................................................................................................

Rate your hike ★ ★ ★ ★ ★

# NOTES AND PICTURES

**TRAIL** ........................................................................... **DATE** ...............

Location ...................................................................................................

Weather ☀ ⛅ ☁ ⛅ 🌧 ⛈ ☁ 🌨 🌨 Temperature ...............

Duration and distance ........................... Time of day ...........................

Type of hike ☐ Loop ☐ Out and back ☐ One way

Terrain ....................................................................................................

Trail conditions ....................................................................................

Other hikers on the trail ☐ Many ☐ Some ☐ Few ☐ None

Difficulty level ☐ Easy ☐ Moderate ☐ Strenuous

Hiking companion(s) .............................................................................

Facilities ................................................................................................

☐ First visit ☐ Return hike ☐ Would hike again

Observations (wildlife, trees and other flora, geology, views, rivers and lakes)

....................................................................................................................

....................................................................................................................

....................................................................................................................

....................................................................................................................

Trail pros and cons ..............................................................................

....................................................................................................................

....................................................................................................................

Things to remember for next time .......................................................

....................................................................................................................

Highlights ..............................................................................................

....................................................................................................................

Rate your hike ★ ★ ★ ★ ★

# NOTES AND PICTURES

**TRAIL** ........................................................................................... **DATE** ...............

Location ...............................................................................................................

Weather ☀ ⛅ ☁ 🌤 🌧 ⛈ 🌥 ☁ 🌨    Temperature ..................

Duration and distance .......................... Time of day ..........................

Type of hike  ☐ Loop   ☐ Out and back   ☐ One way

Terrain ...............................................................................................................

Trail conditions ...............................................................................................

Other hikers on the trail  ☐ Many   ☐ Some   ☐ Few   ☐ None

Difficulty level  ☐ Easy   ☐ Moderate   ☐ Strenuous

Hiking companion(s) .......................................................................................

Facilities ...........................................................................................................

☐ First visit   ☐ Return hike   ☐ Would hike again

Observations (wildlife, trees and other flora, geology, views, rivers and lakes)

...............................................................................................................

...............................................................................................................

...............................................................................................................

Trail pros and cons .........................................................................................

...............................................................................................................

...............................................................................................................

Things to remember for next time ..................................................................

...............................................................................................................

Highlights .........................................................................................................

...............................................................................................................

Rate your hike   ★ ★ ★ ★ ★

# NOTES AND PICTURES

**TRAIL** ............................................................................................ **DATE** ...............

Location ....................................................................................................................

Weather ☀️ ⛅ ☁️ 🌤️ 🌧️ ⛈️ ☁️ 🌨️ 🌨️ Temperature ...............

Duration and distance......................... Time of day.........................

Type of hike  ☐ Loop   ☐ Out and back   ☐ One way

Terrain ......................................................................................................................

Trail conditions ...................................................................................................

Other hikers on the trail  ☐ Many   ☐ Some   ☐ Few   ☐ None

Difficulty level  ☐ Easy   ☐ Moderate   ☐ Strenuous

Hiking companion(s).............................................................................................

Facilities.................................................................................................................

☐ First visit   ☐ Return hike   ☐ Would hike again

Observations (wildlife, trees and other flora, geology, views, rivers and lakes)

....................................................................................................................................

....................................................................................................................................

....................................................................................................................................

Trail pros and cons..............................................................................................

....................................................................................................................................

....................................................................................................................................

Things to remember for next time.....................................................................

....................................................................................................................................

Highlights................................................................................................................

....................................................................................................................................

Rate your hike  ★ ★ ★ ★ ★

# NOTES AND PICTURES

**TRAIL** .................................................................................................. **DATE** ..................

Location ............................................................................................................................

Weather ☀ ⛅ ☁ ⛅ 🌧 ⛈ ☁ ❄ 🌨 Temperature ........................

Duration and distance........................................Time of day ...............................

Type of hike  ☐ Loop  ☐ Out and back  ☐ One way

Terrain ...............................................................................................................................

Trail conditions ...............................................................................................................

Other hikers on the trail  ☐ Many  ☐ Some  ☐ Few  ☐ None

Difficulty level  ☐ Easy  ☐ Moderate  ☐ Strenuous

Hiking companion(s)........................................................................................................

Facilities............................................................................................................................

☐ First visit  ☐ Return hike  ☐ Would hike again

Observations (wildlife, trees and other flora, geology, views, rivers and lakes)

........................................................................................................................................

........................................................................................................................................

........................................................................................................................................

Trail pros and cons........................................................................................................

........................................................................................................................................

........................................................................................................................................

Things to remember for next time.................................................................................

........................................................................................................................................

Highlights.........................................................................................................................

........................................................................................................................................

Rate your hike  ★ ★ ★ ★ ★

# NOTES AND PICTURES

**TRAIL** ............................................................................................ **DATE** ....................

Location .................................................................................................................

Weather ☀ ⛅ ☁ ⛅ 🌧 ⛈ ☁ 🌨 🌨 Temperature ....................

Duration and distance ........................... Time of day ..........................

Type of hike ☐ Loop ☐ Out and back ☐ One way

Terrain ...................................................................................................................

Trail conditions ....................................................................................................

Other hikers on the trail ☐ Many ☐ Some ☐ Few ☐ None

Difficulty level ☐ Easy ☐ Moderate ☐ Strenuous

Hiking companion(s) ..............................................................................................

Facilities ...............................................................................................................

☐ First visit ☐ Return hike ☐ Would hike again

Observations (wildlife, trees and other flora, geology, views, rivers and lakes)

.............................................................................................................................

.............................................................................................................................

.............................................................................................................................

.............................................................................................................................

Trail pros and cons ...............................................................................................

.............................................................................................................................

.............................................................................................................................

Things to remember for next time ........................................................................

.............................................................................................................................

Highlights ............................................................................................................

.............................................................................................................................

Rate your hike ★ ★ ★ ★ ★

# NOTES AND PICTURES

**TRAIL** .................................................................................................... **DATE** ...................

Location .............................................................................................................................

Weather ☀ ⛅ ☁ 🌤 🌦 ⛈ ☁ 🌨 🌨 Temperature ...................

Duration and distance ........................... Time of day ...................................

Type of hike ☐ Loop ☐ Out and back ☐ One way

Terrain ..............................................................................................................................

Trail conditions ...............................................................................................................

Other hikers on the trail ☐ Many ☐ Some ☐ Few ☐ None

Difficulty level ☐ Easy ☐ Moderate ☐ Strenuous

Hiking companion(s) ........................................................................................................

Facilities ...........................................................................................................................

☐ First visit ☐ Return hike ☐ Would hike again

Observations (wildlife, trees and other flora, geology, views, rivers and lakes)

..............................................................................................................................................

..............................................................................................................................................

..............................................................................................................................................

Trail pros and cons ...........................................................................................................

..............................................................................................................................................

..............................................................................................................................................

Things to remember for next time ...................................................................................

..............................................................................................................................................

Highlights ..........................................................................................................................

..............................................................................................................................................

Rate your hike ★ ★ ★ ★ ★

# NOTES AND PICTURES

**TRAIL** .................................................................................. **DATE** ................................

Location ...............................................................................................................

Weather ☀ ⛅ ☁ 🌤 🌧 ⚡ ☁ ❄ 🌨   Temperature ........................

Duration and distance ........................... Time of day ...........................

Type of hike  ☐ Loop   ☐ Out and back   ☐ One way

Terrain ................................................................................................................

Trail conditions ...............................................................................................

Other hikers on the trail  ☐ Many   ☐ Some   ☐ Few   ☐ None

Difficulty level  ☐ Easy   ☐ Moderate   ☐ Strenuous

Hiking companion(s) ........................................................................................

Facilities ...........................................................................................................

☐ First visit   ☐ Return hike   ☐ Would hike again

Observations (wildlife, trees and other flora, geology, views, rivers and lakes)

..........................................................................................................................

..........................................................................................................................

..........................................................................................................................

Trail pros and cons ..........................................................................................

..........................................................................................................................

..........................................................................................................................

Things to remember for next time ...............................................................

..........................................................................................................................

Highlights ..........................................................................................................

..........................................................................................................................

Rate your hike   ★ ★ ★ ★ ★

# NOTES AND PICTURES

**TRAIL** ......................................................................... **DATE** ..............................

Location ..........................................................................................................

Weather ☀ 🌤 ☁ ⛅ 🌧 ⛈ 🌨 ❄ 🌨 Temperature ..............................

Duration and distance........................... Time of day ...................................

Type of hike ☐ Loop ☐ Out and back ☐ One way

Terrain ...........................................................................................................

Trail conditions ...........................................................................................

Other hikers on the trail ☐ Many ☐ Some ☐ Few ☐ None

Difficulty level ☐ Easy ☐ Moderate ☐ Strenuous

Hiking companion(s).....................................................................................

Facilities.........................................................................................................

☐ First visit ☐ Return hike ☐ Would hike again

Observations (wildlife, trees and other flora, geology, views, rivers and lakes)

.........................................................................................................................

.........................................................................................................................

.........................................................................................................................

Trail pros and cons........................................................................................

.........................................................................................................................

.........................................................................................................................

Things to remember for next time................................................................

.........................................................................................................................

Highlights.......................................................................................................

.........................................................................................................................

Rate your hike ★ ★ ★ ★ ★

# NOTES AND PICTURES

**TRAIL** ........................................................................................... **DATE** ..................

Location ......................................................................................................................

Weather ☀️ ⛅ ☁️ 🌤️ 🌧️ ⛈️ ☁️ 🌨️ 🌨️ Temperature ...................

Duration and distance ............................... Time of day ...........................

Type of hike ☐ Loop ☐ Out and back ☐ One way

Terrain ........................................................................................................................

Trail conditions ......................................................................................................

Other hikers on the trail ☐ Many ☐ Some ☐ Few ☐ None

Difficulty level ☐ Easy ☐ Moderate ☐ Strenuous

Hiking companion(s) ..............................................................................................

Facilities .....................................................................................................................

☐ First visit ☐ Return hike ☐ Would hike again

Observations (wildlife, trees and other flora, geology, views, rivers and lakes)

......................................................................................................................................

......................................................................................................................................

......................................................................................................................................

......................................................................................................................................

Trail pros and cons ................................................................................................

......................................................................................................................................

......................................................................................................................................

Things to remember for next time .....................................................................

......................................................................................................................................

Highlights ..................................................................................................................

......................................................................................................................................

Rate your hike ★ ★ ★ ★ ★

# NOTES AND PICTURES

**TRAIL** ........................................................................... **DATE** ..............

Location ......................................................................................

Weather ☀ ⛅ ☁ 🌤 🌧 ⛈ ☁ 🌨 🌨 Temperature ..................

Duration and distance ........................... Time of day ..................

Type of hike ☐ Loop ☐ Out and back ☐ One way

Terrain ........................................................................................

Trail conditions ............................................................................

Other hikers on the trail ☐ Many ☐ Some ☐ Few ☐ None

Difficulty level ☐ Easy ☐ Moderate ☐ Strenuous

Hiking companion(s) ......................................................................

Facilities ......................................................................................

☐ First visit ☐ Return hike ☐ Would hike again

Observations (wildlife, trees and other flora, geology, views, rivers and lakes)

........................................................................................................

........................................................................................................

........................................................................................................

Trail pros and cons ......................................................................

........................................................................................................

........................................................................................................

Things to remember for next time ................................................

........................................................................................................

Highlights ....................................................................................

........................................................................................................

Rate your hike ★ ★ ★ ★ ★

# NOTES AND PICTURES

**TRAIL** ..................................................... **DATE** ..................

Location ...........................................................................

Weather ☀ ⛅ ☁ 🌤 🌦 ⛈ ☁ 🌨 🌨 Temperature ...........

Duration and distance ....................... Time of day ....................

Type of hike ☐ Loop ☐ Out and back ☐ One way

Terrain ...........................................................................

Trail conditions ...........................................................................

Other hikers on the trail ☐ Many ☐ Some ☐ Few ☐ None

Difficulty level ☐ Easy ☐ Moderate ☐ Strenuous

Hiking companion(s) ...........................................................................

Facilities ...........................................................................

☐ First visit ☐ Return hike ☐ Would hike again

Observations (wildlife, trees and other flora, geology, views, rivers and lakes)

...........................................................................

...........................................................................

...........................................................................

...........................................................................

Trail pros and cons ...........................................................................

...........................................................................

...........................................................................

Things to remember for next time ...........................................................................

...........................................................................

Highlights ...........................................................................

...........................................................................

Rate your hike ★ ★ ★ ★ ★

# NOTES AND PICTURES

**TRAIL** ......................................................................................................... **DATE** ...................

Location ...............................................................................................................................

Weather ☀ ⛅ ☁ 🌤 🌥 ⛈ ☁ 🌨 🌨 Temperature ...................

Duration and distance........................................Time of day............................

Type of hike ☐ Loop ☐ Out and back ☐ One way

Terrain ....................................................................................................................

Trail conditions ....................................................................................................

Other hikers on the trail ☐ Many ☐ Some ☐ Few ☐ None

Difficulty level ☐ Easy ☐ Moderate ☐ Strenuous

Hiking companion(s)..............................................................................................

Facilities................................................................................................................

☐ First visit ☐ Return hike ☐ Would hike again

Observations (wildlife, trees and other flora, geology, views, rivers and lakes)

...............................................................................................................................

...............................................................................................................................

...............................................................................................................................

Trail pros and cons................................................................................................

...............................................................................................................................

...............................................................................................................................

Things to remember for next time.........................................................................

...............................................................................................................................

Highlights...............................................................................................................

...............................................................................................................................

Rate your hike ★ ★ ★ ★ ★

# NOTES AND PICTURES

**TRAIL** ................................................................................................ **DATE** ..........................

Location .........................................................................................................................

Weather ☀ ⛅ ☁ 🌤 🌧 ⛈ ☁ 🌨 🌨 Temperature ..........................

Duration and distance........................................ Time of day ..............................

Type of hike ☐ Loop ☐ Out and back ☐ One way

Terrain .........................................................................................................................

Trail conditions ...........................................................................................................

Other hikers on the trail ☐ Many ☐ Some ☐ Few ☐ None

Difficulty level ☐ Easy ☐ Moderate ☐ Strenuous

Hiking companion(s)....................................................................................................

Facilities.......................................................................................................................

☐ First visit ☐ Return hike ☐ Would hike again

Observations (wildlife, trees and other flora, geology, views, rivers and lakes)

.........................................................................................................................

.........................................................................................................................

.........................................................................................................................

Trail pros and cons.....................................................................................................

.........................................................................................................................

.........................................................................................................................

Things to remember for next time.............................................................................

.........................................................................................................................

.........................................................................................................................

Highlights.....................................................................................................................

.........................................................................................................................

Rate your hike ★ ★ ★ ★ ★

# NOTES AND PICTURES

**TRAIL** ............................................................................................ **DATE** ..................

Location .............................................................................................................

Weather ☀ ⛅ ☁ 🌤 🌦 ⛈ 🌥 🌨 🌨 Temperature .................

Duration and distance ........................... Time of day ........................

Type of hike ☐ Loop ☐ Out and back ☐ One way

Terrain ..............................................................................................................

Trail conditions ..............................................................................................

Other hikers on the trail ☐ Many ☐ Some ☐ Few ☐ None

Difficulty level ☐ Easy ☐ Moderate ☐ Strenuous

Hiking companion(s) .......................................................................................

Facilities ..........................................................................................................

☐ First visit ☐ Return hike ☐ Would hike again

Observations (wildlife, trees and other flora, geology, views, rivers and lakes)

..............................................................................................................................

..............................................................................................................................

..............................................................................................................................

Trail pros and cons ........................................................................................

..............................................................................................................................

..............................................................................................................................

Things to remember for next time ...............................................................

..............................................................................................................................

Highlights ........................................................................................................

..............................................................................................................................

Rate your hike  ★ ★ ★ ★ ★

# NOTES AND PICTURES

**TRAIL** ................................................................................................ **DATE** ........................

Location ................................................................................................................

Weather ☀ ⛅ ☁ 🌤 🌧 ⛈ ☁ 🌨 🌨 Temperature ........................

Duration and distance ........................................ Time of day ........................

Type of hike ☐ Loop ☐ Out and back ☐ One way

Terrain ................................................................................................................

Trail conditions ........................................................................................

Other hikers on the trail ☐ Many ☐ Some ☐ Few ☐ None

Difficulty level ☐ Easy ☐ Moderate ☐ Strenuous

Hiking companion(s) ........................................................................

Facilities ................................................................................................

☐ First visit ☐ Return hike ☐ Would hike again

Observations (wildlife, trees and other flora, geology, views, rivers and lakes)

................................................................................................................

................................................................................................................

................................................................................................................

Trail pros and cons ........................................................................

................................................................................................................

................................................................................................................

Things to remember for next time ........................................................

................................................................................................................

Highlights ................................................................................................

................................................................................................................

Rate your hike ★ ★ ★ ★ ★

# NOTES AND PICTURES

**TRAIL** .................................................................... **DATE** ..............................

Location ........................................................................................................

Weather ☀ ⛅ ☁ ⛅ 🌧 ⛈ ☁ 🌨 🌨 Temperature ...................

Duration and distance ..............................Time of day ..............................

Type of hike  ☐ Loop    ☐ Out and back    ☐ One way

Terrain ........................................................................................................

Trail conditions ........................................................................................

Other hikers on the trail  ☐ Many   ☐ Some   ☐ Few   ☐ None

Difficulty level  ☐ Easy   ☐ Moderate   ☐ Strenuous

Hiking companion(s) ................................................................................

Facilities ....................................................................................................

☐ First visit   ☐ Return hike   ☐ Would hike again

Observations (wildlife, trees and other flora, geology, views, rivers and lakes)

........................................................................................................

........................................................................................................

........................................................................................................

Trail pros and cons ..................................................................................

........................................................................................................

........................................................................................................

Things to remember for next time ...........................................................

........................................................................................................

Highlights ..................................................................................................

........................................................................................................

Rate your hike   ★  ★  ★  ★  ★

# NOTES AND PICTURES

**TRAIL** ............................................................................................ **DATE** ...............................

Location ........................................................................................................................

Weather ☀ ⛅ ☁ 🌤 🌧 ⛈ 🌥 🌨 🌨 Temperature ...........................

Duration and distance ................................ Time of day ...........................................

Type of hike ☐ Loop  ☐ Out and back  ☐ One way

Terrain .........................................................................................................................

Trail conditions .........................................................................................................

Other hikers on the trail ☐ Many  ☐ Some  ☐ Few  ☐ None

Difficulty level ☐ Easy  ☐ Moderate  ☐ Strenuous

Hiking companion(s) ...................................................................................................

Facilities ......................................................................................................................

☐ First visit  ☐ Return hike  ☐ Would hike again

Observations (wildlife, trees and other flora, geology, views, rivers and lakes)

........................................................................................................................................

........................................................................................................................................

........................................................................................................................................

Trail pros and cons ....................................................................................................

........................................................................................................................................

........................................................................................................................................

Things to remember for next time ...........................................................................

........................................................................................................................................

Highlights ....................................................................................................................

........................................................................................................................................

Rate your hike ★ ★ ★ ★ ★

# NOTES AND PICTURES

**TRAIL** .................................................................................. **DATE** ..............................

Location ............................................................................................................

Weather ☀ ⛈ ☁ ⛅ 🌧 ⚡ ☁ ❄ 🌨 Temperature ......................

Duration and distance ........................... Time of day ...............................

Type of hike ☐ Loop ☐ Out and back ☐ One way

Terrain ...............................................................................................................

Trail conditions .................................................................................................

Other hikers on the trail ☐ Many ☐ Some ☐ Few ☐ None

Difficulty level ☐ Easy ☐ Moderate ☐ Strenuous

Hiking companion(s) ...........................................................................................

Facilities ...........................................................................................................

☐ First visit ☐ Return hike ☐ Would hike again

Observations (wildlife, trees and other flora, geology, views, rivers and lakes)

................................................................................................................................

................................................................................................................................

................................................................................................................................

................................................................................................................................

Trail pros and cons ...........................................................................................

................................................................................................................................

................................................................................................................................

Things to remember for next time ...................................................................

................................................................................................................................

Highlights ........................................................................................................

................................................................................................................................

Rate your hike ★ ★ ★ ★ ★

# NOTES AND PICTURES

**TRAIL** ............................................................................................ **DATE** ................

Location ...........................................................................................................

Weather ☀ ⛅ ☁ 🌤 🌧 ⛈ ☁ 🌨 🌨 Temperature ................

Duration and distance ........................... Time of day ...................

Type of hike ☐ Loop ☐ Out and back ☐ One way

Terrain ............................................................................................................

Trail conditions .............................................................................................

Other hikers on the trail ☐ Many ☐ Some ☐ Few ☐ None

Difficulty level ☐ Easy ☐ Moderate ☐ Strenuous

Hiking companion(s) .......................................................................................

Facilities .........................................................................................................

☐ First visit ☐ Return hike ☐ Would hike again

Observations (wildlife, trees and other flora, geology, views, rivers and lakes)

...........................................................................................................

...........................................................................................................

...........................................................................................................

Trail pros and cons .........................................................................................

...........................................................................................................

...........................................................................................................

Things to remember for next time ....................................................................

...........................................................................................................

Highlights .......................................................................................................

...........................................................................................................

Rate your hike ★ ★ ★ ★ ★

# NOTES AND PICTURES

**TRAIL** ........................................................................................................ **DATE** ......................

Location ...............................................................................................................................

Weather ☀ ⛅ ☁ 🌤 🌧 ⚡ ☁ 🌨 🌨 Temperature ......................

Duration and distance ...................................... Time of day ......................................

Type of hike ☐ Loop ☐ Out and back ☐ One way

Terrain ...................................................................................................................

Trail conditions ......................................................................................................

Other hikers on the trail ☐ Many ☐ Some ☐ Few ☐ None

Difficulty level ☐ Easy ☐ Moderate ☐ Strenuous

Hiking companion(s) ...............................................................................................

Facilities ...............................................................................................................

☐ First visit ☐ Return hike ☐ Would hike again

Observations (wildlife, trees and other flora, geology, views, rivers and lakes)

...........................................................................................................................

...........................................................................................................................

...........................................................................................................................

Trail pros and cons ................................................................................................

...........................................................................................................................

...........................................................................................................................

Things to remember for next time .........................................................................

...........................................................................................................................

Highlights .............................................................................................................

...........................................................................................................................

Rate your hike ★ ★ ★ ★ ★

# NOTES AND PICTURES

**TRAIL** ..................................................................................................... **DATE** ...................

Location ........................................................................................................................................

Weather ☀ ⛆ ☁ ⛅ ☁ ⛈ ☁ ☁ Temperature ...................

Duration and distance ..................................... Time of day ..............................................

Type of hike  ☐ Loop    ☐ Out and back    ☐ One way

Terrain ..........................................................................................................................................

Trail conditions .........................................................................................................................

Other hikers on the trail  ☐ Many  ☐ Some  ☐ Few  ☐ None

Difficulty level  ☐ Easy  ☐ Moderate  ☐ Strenuous

Hiking companion(s) ...............................................................................................................

Facilities ......................................................................................................................................

☐ First visit    ☐ Return hike    ☐ Would hike again

Observations (wildlife, trees and other flora, geology, views, rivers and lakes)

........................................................................................................................................................

........................................................................................................................................................

........................................................................................................................................................

Trail pros and cons ..................................................................................................................

........................................................................................................................................................

........................................................................................................................................................

Things to remember for next time ..................................................................................

........................................................................................................................................................

Highlights ...................................................................................................................................

........................................................................................................................................................

Rate your hike  ★ ★ ★ ★ ★

# NOTES AND PICTURES

**TRAIL** ............................................................................................ **DATE** ...............

Location ...............................................................................................................

Weather ☀ ⛅ ☁ 🌤 🌧 ⛈ 🌧 🌨 🌨 Temperature .......................

Duration and distance........................ Time of day ...................................

Type of hike  ☐ Loop  ☐ Out and back  ☐ One way

Terrain ..................................................................................................................

Trail conditions ..................................................................................................

Other hikers on the trail  ☐ Many  ☐ Some  ☐ Few  ☐ None

Difficulty level  ☐ Easy  ☐ Moderate  ☐ Strenuous

Hiking companion(s)............................................................................................

Facilities...............................................................................................................

☐ First visit  ☐ Return hike  ☐ Would hike again

Observations (wildlife, trees and other flora, geology, views, rivers and lakes)

.............................................................................................................................

.............................................................................................................................

.............................................................................................................................

Trail pros and cons............................................................................................

.............................................................................................................................

.............................................................................................................................

Things to remember for next time....................................................................

.............................................................................................................................

Highlights.............................................................................................................

.............................................................................................................................

Rate your hike  ★ ★ ★ ★ ★

# NOTES AND PICTURES

**TRAIL** .............................................................................................. **DATE** ......................

Location ............................................................................................................................

Weather ☀ ⛅ ☁ 🌤 🌧 ⛈ 🌧 🌨 🌨 Temperature ..................

Duration and distance .......................... Time of day ..............................................

Type of hike  ☐ Loop   ☐ Out and back   ☐ One way

Terrain ..............................................................................................................................

Trail conditions ..............................................................................................................

Other hikers on the trail  ☐ Many   ☐ Some   ☐ Few   ☐ None

Difficulty level  ☐ Easy   ☐ Moderate   ☐ Strenuous

Hiking companion(s) .......................................................................................................

Facilities .........................................................................................................................

☐ First visit   ☐ Return hike   ☐ Would hike again

Observations (wildlife, trees and other flora, geology, views, rivers and lakes)

.............................................................................................................................................

.............................................................................................................................................

.............................................................................................................................................

Trail pros and cons ........................................................................................................

.............................................................................................................................................

.............................................................................................................................................

Things to remember for next time .................................................................................

.............................................................................................................................................

Highlights .........................................................................................................................

.............................................................................................................................................

Rate your hike   ★ ★ ★ ★ ★

# NOTES AND PICTURES

**TRAIL** .............................................................................................. **DATE** ..........................

Location ..................................................................................................................

Weather ☀️ ⛅ ☁️ 🌦️ 🌥️ ⛈️ 🌧️ ☁️ 🌨️ Temperature ..............................

Duration and distance .........................................Time of day ...............................

Type of hike ☐ Loop  ☐ Out and back  ☐ One way

Terrain ....................................................................................................................

Trail conditions ......................................................................................................

Other hikers on the trail ☐ Many  ☐ Some  ☐ Few  ☐ None

Difficulty level ☐ Easy  ☐ Moderate  ☐ Strenuous

Hiking companion(s) ...............................................................................................

Facilities ..................................................................................................................

☐ First visit  ☐ Return hike  ☐ Would hike again

Observations (wildlife, trees and other flora, geology, views, rivers and lakes)

............................................................................................................................

............................................................................................................................

............................................................................................................................

............................................................................................................................

Trail pros and cons ................................................................................................

............................................................................................................................

............................................................................................................................

Things to remember for next time ........................................................................

............................................................................................................................

Highlights ................................................................................................................

............................................................................................................................

Rate your hike  ★ ★ ★ ★ ★

# NOTES AND PICTURES

**TRAIL** ........................................................................................................ **DATE** ............................

Location ......................................................................................................................................

Weather ☀ ⛅ ☁ 🌤 🌧 ⛈ ☁ 🌨 🌨 Temperature ....................

Duration and distance........................................Time of day ......................................

Type of hike    ☐ Loop    ☐ Out and back    ☐ One way

Terrain ......................................................................................................................................

Trail conditions ......................................................................................................................

Other hikers on the trail    ☐ Many    ☐ Some    ☐ Few    ☐ None

Difficulty level    ☐ Easy    ☐ Moderate    ☐ Strenuous

Hiking companion(s)..............................................................................................................

Facilities.................................................................................................................................

☐ First visit    ☐ Return hike    ☐ Would hike again

Observations (wildlife, trees and other flora, geology, views, rivers and lakes)

.............................................................................................................................................

.............................................................................................................................................

.............................................................................................................................................

Trail pros and cons..............................................................................................................

.............................................................................................................................................

.............................................................................................................................................

Things to remember for next time......................................................................................

.............................................................................................................................................

Highlights...............................................................................................................................

.............................................................................................................................................

Rate your hike    ★ ★ ★ ★ ★

# NOTES AND PICTURES

**TRAIL** ......................................................................................... **DATE** ..................

Location .........................................................................................................

Weather ☀ ⛅ ☁ ⛅ 🌧 ⛈ ☁ 🌨 🌧 Temperature ..................

Duration and distance ............................ Time of day ..........................

Type of hike ☐ Loop ☐ Out and back ☐ One way

Terrain .........................................................................................................

Trail conditions ..........................................................................................

Other hikers on the trail ☐ Many ☐ Some ☐ Few ☐ None

Difficulty level ☐ Easy ☐ Moderate ☐ Strenuous

Hiking companion(s) ..................................................................................

Facilities ......................................................................................................

☐ First visit ☐ Return hike ☐ Would hike again

Observations (wildlife, trees and other flora, geology, views, rivers and lakes)

..........................................................................................................................

..........................................................................................................................

..........................................................................................................................

Trail pros and cons ..................................................................................

..........................................................................................................................

..........................................................................................................................

Things to remember for next time ..........................................................

..........................................................................................................................

Highlights ..................................................................................................

..........................................................................................................................

Rate your hike ★ ★ ★ ★ ★

# NOTES AND PICTURES

**TRAIL** .................................................................................................... **DATE** ..........................

Location ..................................................................................................................................

Weather ☀ ⛅ ☁ 🌤 🌦 ⛈ ☁ 🌨 🌧 Temperature ..........................

Duration and distance........................................Time of day..........................

Type of hike  ☐ Loop   ☐ Out and back   ☐ One way

Terrain ......................................................................................................................

Trail conditions ......................................................................................................

Other hikers on the trail  ☐ Many  ☐ Some  ☐ Few  ☐ None

Difficulty level  ☐ Easy  ☐ Moderate  ☐ Strenuous

Hiking companion(s).............................................................................................

Facilities................................................................................................................

☐ First visit  ☐ Return hike  ☐ Would hike again

Observations (wildlife, trees and other flora, geology, views, rivers and lakes)

.............................................................................................................................

.............................................................................................................................

.............................................................................................................................

Trail pros and cons...............................................................................................

.............................................................................................................................

.............................................................................................................................

Things to remember for next time.......................................................................

.............................................................................................................................

Highlights...............................................................................................................

.............................................................................................................................

Rate your hike  ★ ★ ★ ★ ★

# NOTES AND PICTURES

# HIKING TIPS

◆ Pack essentials for day hikers (but keep it light):

- ○ Map and compass
- ○ Sunglasses and travel-size sunscreen
- ○ Extra clothing: waterproof/windproof jacket, hat, extra layers, and socks
- ○ Headlamp or flashlight
- ○ First-aid supplies, including blister treatment
- ○ Bug repellent
- ○ Pocket knife
- ○ Waterproof matches or lighter and candle
- ○ Mylar blanket
- ○ Repair kit and tools
- ○ Food and water (at least 1/2 liter per person per hour)

◆ Check the weather before hiking to minimize unpleasant surprises and to prepare for conditions.

◆ Familiarize yourself with local flora and fauna that may be hazardous, and take precautions. If you're in an area with ticks, wear long pants, tuck your pant legs into your socks, and check yourself for ticks post-hike. If there's poison ivy, ash, or oak around, learn what it looks like so that you can avoid it.

◆ Dress for success: comfortable footwear, hiking socks, moisture-wicking clothes.

◆ Match your fitness level to your hike, figuring an average of 2 miles per hour (3 km/hour) for average fitness on level terrain.

◆ Check a trail map to note possibly tricky trail intersections, overlooks, lunch spots, and other features. If no paper map is available, take a photo of a posted map.

◆ Hike with a partner, and/or tell someone else where you're going.

◆ Stay on trails to preserve vegetation.

◆ Drink water from lakes or rivers only after treating it first (boiling, filtering, or using purification tablets).

◆ Follow good hikers' etiquette:

- ○ Hikers going downhill should yield to hikers going uphill.
- ○ Hikers on foot bridges have the right of way.
- ○ Keep dogs under control.
- ○ Appreciate wildlife, but don't feed it.

◆ Soak up the fresh air and natural beauty!

◆ Add your own: ..............................................................................................................................

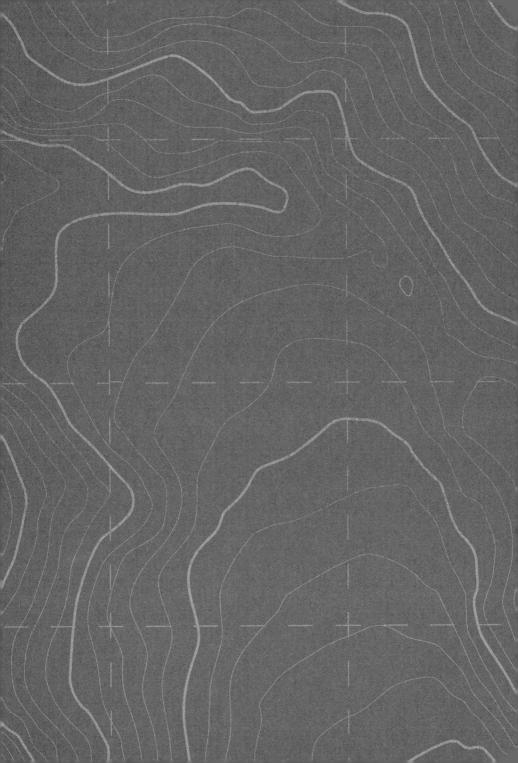